Everything You Need To Know About
STEPFAMILIES

The new members of a stepfamily often feel strange. They need time to adjust.

Everything You Need To Know About

STEP-FAMILIES

Bruce Glassman

Series Editor: Evan Stark, Ph.D.

THE ROSEN PUBLISHING GROUP, INC.
NEW YORK

Published in 1988, 1991, 1994 by The Rosen Publishing Group, Inc.
29 East 21st Street, New York, NY 10010

Revised Edition 1994
Copyright 1988, 1991, 1994 by The Rosen Publishing Group, Inc.

Manufactured in the United States of America.

Library of Congress Cataloging-in-Publication Data

Glassman, Bruce
    Everything you need to know about stepfamilies.
    (The Need to know library)
    Includes bibliographical references and index.
    Summary: Discusses the problems and adjustments
involved in having only one parent in the family and
what happens when that parent remarries, giving the
child a stepfamily.
ISBN 0-8239-1798-3
    1. Stepfamilies—United States—Juvenile literature.
2. Children of single parents—United States—Juvenile
literature. [1. Stepfamilies. 2. Single-parent family.
3. Remarriage] I. Title. II. Series.
HQ759.92.G57   1993
306.8'74   88-24022
                                                CIP
                                                AC

Contents

Introduction

In the 1950s, most people thought of a "typical" family as one with a mother, father, two children, and a big friendly dog. But this idea has changed greatly since then. Today, there are so many kinds of families that calling any one particular kind "typical" is very misleading.

Families headed by a biological mother and father are still very common. But so are single-parent families and adoptive families. Then there are foster families and extended families (where parents, children, and other relatives live together). There are also homosexual families (headed by two adults of the same sex) and communal families (where related and nonrelated people share a home). But one kind of family that you may already be familiar with is the stepfamily or "blended" family. This kind of family blends members from previous families together.

Of all the kinds of families, stepfamilies are becoming the most common. Each day about 1,300 stepfamilies are formed. One out of every six children is a stepchild.

Stepfamilies are formed for a number of different reasons. Sometimes a parent dies. Sometimes parents get divorced. Remarriage after divorce is the most common way stepfamilies are formed.

Stepfamilies have been around for a long time. Even the Pilgrims in the 1600s had stepfamilies. And some of the world's best-known leaders lived in stepfamilies. Did you know that George Washington, Abraham Lincoln, and Ronald Reagan were each part of a stepfamily?

Today, there is a growing increase in the number of divorces and remarriages. To reflect the changes in our society, Hollywood movies and television shows are producing more stories about different kinds of stepfamilies than ever before.

This book is about how stepfamilies are formed and how the people within them must adapt to new living situations. Stepfamily members often expect a great deal from the new family unit and from one another. Sometimes these expectations are not reasonable. Unfair expectations may lead to disappointment and unhappiness. This book will talk about some ways to avoid that unhappiness by being more realistic.

Most important, this book will show that stepfamilies are unique in many ways. They have both strengths *and* weaknesses. When the members of a stepfamily learn to appreciate what makes their family special, they are best able to love and care for one another in the most satisfying way.

A child and a single parent often help each other cope with big changes in a family.

Chapter 1

Living with a Single Parent

Most stepfamilies are formed after children live in a single-parent family for a while. The most common factor that creates single-parent families is divorce.

There are more single-parent families today than ever before. In fact, as the number of families with children has increased in recent years, so has the number of single-parent families. Between 1980 and 1990, the number of families with two parents and children remained unchanged for the most part. But single-parent families increased by over 40 percent. Today, about 3 out of every 10 families are headed by a single parent. That means there are about 10 million single-parent families in America today. By the year 2000, it is estimated that half of all children will have lived in a single-parent family for some time in their lives. As single-parent statistics increase, so do those for stepfamilies.

Life in a single-parent family is often very different from life in a stepfamily. Single parents and children may have adjusted well to living with just each other. But then a stepfamily is formed and everyone must adapt to new changes. A number of things can make adapting difficult.

Fearing the loss of your special bond. The death of a parent or a divorce is a painful time for everyone in a family. You and your single parent will bond more strongly as you cope with this situation together. But when a stepparent comes along, you may feel threatened. You may be afraid that you and your parent will not remain as close as you had been in the past.

Sharing your parent's attention. Before there was someone else in your parent's life, you had all the attention. But with someone new, you must share that attention. For many people, this will feel like a loss. Sharing attention is not always a bad thing. If you try, you can make any time you spend with your parent feel special. All it takes is the right attitude—a willingness to try.

Seeing your parent in love again. Being around people who are hugging and kissing all the time can be awkward. You may feel particularly uncomfortable about seeing your parent being

affectionate with someone you still think of as a
"stranger." These feelings are perfectly normal.
But it is also normal for your parent to want adult
companionship. Try to understand that happy new
relationships will make everyone happier in the
long run. Even you!

> Dear Diary,
> I am gonna barf. Dad's new girlfriend is totally gross.
> Every time she comes over she holds my dad's hand.
> And then she asks him to kiss her all the time. It's
> gross. I wish I didn't have to see that stuff around the
> house.
>
> Alberto, age 12

Seeing your parent "in love" may make you feel
sick. It probably embarrasses you when you see
your parent giggling with a lover or a date. Flirting
and holding hands may annoy you. You aren't sure
how to act. It's possible that you have never seen
your parent act this way. Maybe it wasn't like this
with your natural parents.

New rules. Rules seem to be changing all the
time. You had rules in your old family. Then you
had new rules in your single-parent family. Now
the rules have probably changed again. All these
changes can make you feel upset and out of control. But rules change as situations change. And
accepting change is one of the most important
parts of living in a new family.

Jumping to conclusions. Because things in your life have been changing so much, you may feel ready for something to last. You want a feeling of security. But counting on things too soon can lead to disappointment. Try to be patient. New relationships need enough time to work.

> Dear Diary,
> Dad's got the coolest new girlfriend. He says she knows how to cook and how to fix bikes. Tonight was their second date. I think it's gonna be serious. She really likes Dad. And Dad really likes her. I hope they get married. It would be great to have a real family again.
>
> Felicia, age 14

You may want your parent to find another person right away. You may be eager to have a "whole family" again. But you may be expecting too much. You may expect things to go much faster than they can. Then you are disappointed. And then you become angry. You can avoid that. You just need to be patient. You need to give your parent time to get to know the new person.

Feeling Jealous of "Perfect Families"

You may live with a single parent or in a stepfamily. Sometimes, you may look at other families and think they are happier and better off. You may wish you were part of another family. But no family is perfect. Although you may not be

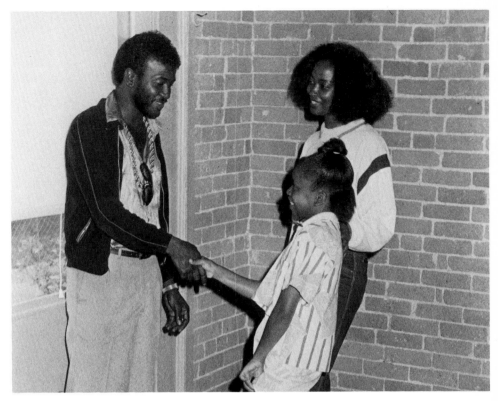
Single parents need to meet new people in order to be happy.

aware of it, every family has problems of its own
to work out. Being jealous only makes you feel
worse. You don't spend enough time learning to
appreciate the good things about your new family.

THINK ABOUT YOUR FEELINGS
1. Does your single parent have a girlfriend or
   boyfriend? Have you told your parent how you
   feel about it?
2. Do you look at your friends' families and wish
   you were part of another family? Do you feel
   jealous about how "perfect" everyone else's
   family seems? Have you asked your friends
   about problems in their families?

13

Remarriage can be a difficult time. Even a wedding can make new stepchildren unhappy.

Chapter 2

Creating a Stepfamily

If you have recently become part of a stepfamily you probably feel many different feelings. You may feel a mix of happiness and anger. You may feel anxious about the future. And you may think that no one else really understands how you feel. But you are not alone. Kids in new stepfamilies are more and more common in the world today.

The Facts on Stepfamilies Today

About 1,300 new stepfamilies form each day. That means about one out of every six children is a stepchild. In 1990, 5.3 million married-couple households had at least one stepchild. By the year 2000, it is estimated that more children will be part of a stepfamily than any other kind of family.

Confused Feelings

Getting remarried should be a happy time for
everyone. It means your parent has found new
love. It means a new family can be formed. But it
can also feel like a terrible time for you. And feeling sad or angry when others are so happy can
make your feelings even worse.

Feeling confused and upset is not unusual.
There is a lot for you to get used to. It probably
seems that you have no control over anything. And
it probably seems that everything is happening way
too fast. You have a whole new family to meet. You
may have new stepbrothers or stepsisters to get to
know. You may even have to think about moving to
a new town and going to a new school.

A new marriage usually involves much planning
and attention. A remarriage often does not give
children a chance to show their true feelings. Your
parent and family will be very busy with their own
feelings at this time. They may not have given your
feelings much thought. This lack of attention can
hurt. And it's another reason why remarriage can
be a difficult time.

A Stepfamily Is Not Like a First Family

Stepfamilies are different from first families.
That is important to remember. It does not mean
they are better. Nor does it mean they are worse.
It just means they are different in some important
ways. Think about the following.

Kids already exist. In a first family the parents usually have some time together as a couple before they have children. They can get to know each other. They can be alone all the time. It is different in a stepfamily. You already exist and perhaps your parent's new spouse has children from another marriage as well. Your parents' new relationship will be different. Your parents will have less time for each other and more responsibility. And that can affect how the marriage develops.

Loyalties may be different. There are no questions of loyalty in a first family. The father is the only father. The mother is the only mother. It is that way from the beginning. But stepfamilies are different. Often a natural parent is living. And that parent is not part of your new family. The question of loyalty arises. You may feel guilty about living in a family that does not include your absent parent. The absent parent may not have remarried and may be more lonely. You may feel guilty even if that parent has died. You may still feel a strong connection to his or her memory.

Sense of belonging. In a first family it is easier to feel that you belong. There is one home. Both your parents are there. But in a stepfamily those feelings of belonging are not always present. Sometimes you must live in a new house in a new place. You have new relatives. These things often do not feel "real." You may not feel that you "belong" with these new things.

Getting Used to New Parents and Privacy

Maybe your single parent will get remarried. Or maybe your parent will have someone move in. If your parent has a new love, you will probably have to give them time to be alone together. That is called *privacy*. Privacy is important for many reasons. Privacy allows a new relationship to grow. And it provides time and space for the sexual side of a relationship. Sexuality is important to a new and growing relationship. It may be hard for you to give your parent time to be alone with his or her new love. You may feel deserted. Or it may feel strange to know that your parent is having sex with someone new. But you must allow the new relationship to become strong. And that means having patience and understanding.

Problems with Names and Titles

Names are very important. They are important in the world. They are important in families. What we call a person shows how we feel about him or her. Or how well we know the person. If a child calls an adult by his or her first name or nickname, they are probably friendly and comfortable with each other. Names also tell other people about relationships. They tell a stranger who your parent is. They tell everyone who *you* are.

In a stepfamily the question of names needs to be given some thought. There really is no right or

After a time, the stepparent may be called "Mom" or "Dad."

wrong choice. Each family member will have an opinion. And it is important for adults to remember that children may feel uncomfortable and unwilling to make a change of this kind too quickly.

Dear Diary,
Stepfamilies are confusing sometimes! Now Roberta wants me to call her "Mom." But I've always called her just "Roberta." I don't wanna call her "Mom." I mean, I like her and everything. And I don't want to hurt her feelings. But she's not my mom. I have a *real* mom in Atlanta. And she wouldn't want me to call Roberta "Mom." How do I have two "moms?"

Roger, age 14

Your stepparent may ask you to use "Mom" or "Dad." But this cannot be forced. You may feel that you are being disloyal to your natural parent if you call your stepparent "Mom" or "Dad." It is confusing. You love your natural parents. You may also love your stepparent, but you may want to keep the title "stepchild" to show that you are not related naturally to the stepparent.

On the other hand, you may want to be called a son or a daughter. You may be anxious to be fully accepted by a new adult. The members of your stepfamily should talk to one another about names. You need to tell one another openly and honestly what each of you wants to be called. Then there is no guessing, no hurt feelings. Whatever name or title that is comfortable for *both* you and your stepparent is best. Decisions in any family must come from feelings of love and respect. And just like love and respect, if they are forced, they will mean nothing.

> Dear Diary,
> It was my first Thanksgiving with Dad and Maria. We went to Maria's parents' house. Her whole family was there. She introduced me to everyone as "Enrico's son." That made me feel bad. I thought we were all one big family now. I thought she would call me her son. I wanted to feel a part of the family. I wanted Maria to say I was her son to everybody else.
>
> Juan, age 11

Changing Last Names

Many times stepchildren do not know what to do about last names. You may live with a natural parent and a stepparent. The natural parent may be your mother. She may change her name. She may take your stepfather's name. Then you are the only one with a different name and may feel a little "left out."

Some children like to take the stepfather's name. They want to feel like part of the new family. Or they want to have the same last name as their mother. But you do not have to change your name. You may feel that it is not your "real" name and you want the connection with your other natural parent to remain. Some people solve the problem by using both last names. For example, Emily Ross who becomes the stepchild of Harold Miller, could hyphenate a new last name and then be called Emily Ross-Miller.

Remember, names tell other people *who* you are, not *what* you are. They are used to identify people. No one name is "better" than another.

The Adoption Option

Some families feel that legal adoption of the stepchildren is a good idea. You may agree to take your stepparent's name. Certain things become easier with adoption. You can use your parents' name at school. With adoption, you are legally related to your stepparent. Adoption makes some

children feel more secure. You may feel that you
would be safe if something happened to your natural parent. If you were adopted, your stepparent
would be legally responsible for you.

Sometimes adoption is best, especially if the
other natural parent is dead, or very far away, or
not regularly in touch. You may also be happy to
take another name if you are not close to or fond
of your absent natural parent.

Holidays and Extended Families

Holidays can be some of the happiest times for a
stepfamily. But they can also be some of the saddest. Often, holidays focus on the idea of "being
one big happy family." People get very excited
about holidays. They want to feel really good during the celebrations. They like to be around the
people they care about the most. Sometimes being
in a stepfamily is a bit of a letdown. You may have

Liz Thompson
19 Park Road
Watkins Glen, PA 14890

Ms. Joan Smith-Stern
4056 Cedar Street
Rockville, MD. 20851

expected to *feel* more like a family than you do. Or maybe you keep comparing your present holidays to ones you had in the past. These are just some examples of expectations that can make you feel unhappy. Remember, it can take a long time for the members of your immediate stepfamily to adjust to one another. It takes even longer for other members of the family to adjust. And in the meantime, they may not remember what you want to be called or what your favorite things are. They may even be shy. You all need time to learn more about one another and decide how you really feel.

Unfair Expectations

Unfair expectations happen when people think something will be better than it can be. Sometimes these are called "fixed ideas." They can cause a lot of unhappiness in stepfamilies. People can fool themselves into believing what they want. But life will not be perfect, and neither will your new family.

• *Expecting Instant Love.*

Dear Diary,
Martin keeps saying "I love you" to me. But he's only been married to Mom for a few months. I mean, he's okay. I like him and I'm glad that Mom is happy. But I feel like he expects me to say "I love you" back. But I don't feel it. I guess he's trying to be like my dad. But I don't want him to be my dad. I want him to be Martin. Am I being bad by not loving my own stepfather?

Donna, age 13

Stepparents cannot win love and trust with presents. It takes time for these feelings to grow.

Stepparents often want you to love them right away. They also want to love you right away. You may feel this as pressure. You may feel that you *have to* love your new parent right away. This is an unfair expectation. IT IS OKAY IF YOU DON'T. It is not natural to force feelings. Especially feelings of love. If the stepfamily works out, the love may come in time.

Many stepparents hardly even know their stepchildren at first. How can they love them right away? Real love is based on respect and trust. These feelings take time to grow.

Your stepparent may try too hard to win your affection. He or she may be overly anxious for "a loving family." This is often difficult for you. Your stepparent may think it will help to shower you with presents. Or to give you a lot of attention. But that is only putting more pressure on you.

- *Thinking of Stepparents as Your "Replacement Parents."*

Your stepparent may think that he or she should replace your parent who has died or moved away. He or she may try hard to act the same way and to do the same things. But no one can replace your parent. No one should be expected to.

Stepparents should be themselves. They should be comfortable with giving their own strengths to a new family. They should not ask you to think of them as substitutes for your absent parent. And you should not compare them to your other parent.

Stepparents should be thought of as additional parents, not replacements.

- *Feeling That You Need to Forget the Absent Parent*

Divorced parents often feel anger toward their former spouse. They are often angry for a long time. Because of this, you might be told to forget your absent parent, that he or she was no good. Or maybe that parent is never mentioned around the house. This is what happens when one parent holds a grudge. It is not fair to you.

You still feel love and loyalty for your absent parent. Those feelings should always be respected and they should not be ignored.

The absent parent is often left out of plans. He or she is forgotten at holidays. It can be very difficult for you to make plans with one parent without the help of the other. But when divorced parents are angry at each other they do not cooperate. And the children suffer.

Name-calling

It is hard for you to hear your parent speak badly about your other (biological) parent. Name-calling and blaming come from anger. They are done to let out frustration (a feeling of helplessness). But it is not your anger and frustration. And it may upset you when you hear it. Parents have a right to be angry. But they must understand that you may not share their anger.

Feeling Pushed Aside by Stepparents

Dear Diary,
What happened to all the time Mom and I spent to-gether? Now she spends all her time with Jermaine.
And I don't get to go to the movies with her anymore.
I wish Jermaine would leave so Mom and I could be together again.

Alicia, age 13

When parents remarry they feel that they are starting over. But you feel it as a loss. You feel you are losing the parent to someone else. That may make you very angry. But you should try to understand that your parent and stepparent are trying to find happiness for themselves and for you.

Discipline by a Stepparent

Every stepfamily starts with changes. They are not necessarily bad. They are not necessarily good. They are just different.

When you become part of a new family, you may have to get used to new rules. Chances are you will accept or reject these new rules depending on your feelings for your stepparent.

It is not fair to expect your stepparent to think exactly the same way your natural parent does. It is also unfair for a stepparent to demand completely new behavior from you now that he or she is part of your family.

THINK ABOUT YOUR FEELINGS

1. Do you feel pushed aside by your real parent? Have you told your parent that you miss his/her company? Can you and your parent agree on when you can spend time together?

2. What are your expectations for your stepfamily? Do you want everything to "work out" right away? Are you being patient with your stepparent? Is he/she being patient with you?

Chapter 3

When Divorce Changes a Family

Only a few decades ago, divorce was fairly rare in America. Husbands and wives tended to stay together for economic, religious, or social reasons—even if they were unhappy. People in society often thought badly of people who were divorced. Today, however, divorce is quite common. Roughly half of all marriages end in divorce. In 1991 alone, about 1.2 million people got divorced. Society no longer regards divorced people as "failures."

What does all this divorce mean? It means there are more and more people getting remarried. And that means more and more stepfamilies are being created.

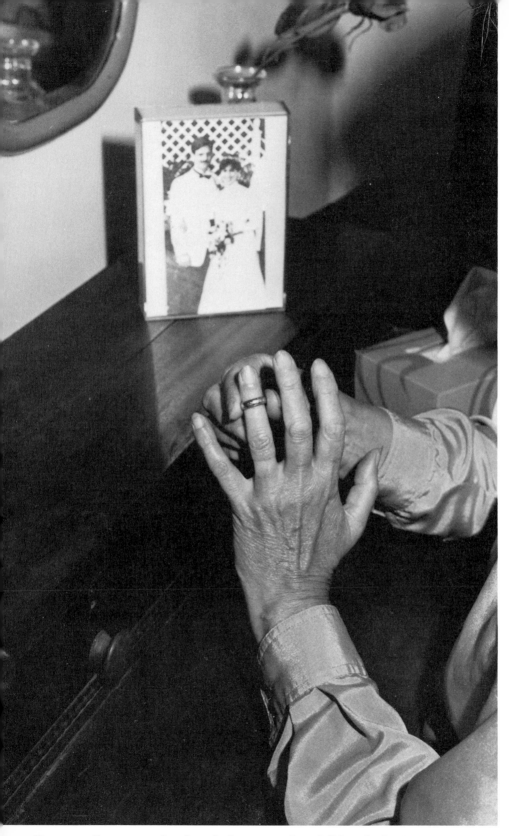

Parents divorce *each other*. It is never the children's fault.

Why Do Parents Divorce?

Parents divorce for many reasons. Many times, they have emotional conflicts with each other that make them both unhappy. Other times, outside influences put strains on a marriage. Children in unhappy families often think that problems and divorce are actually their fault. But that is never true. Parents do not divorce because of anything their children do.

The circumstances of each divorce are as unique as each marriage. But there are some common reasons that parents often give for their unhappiness. Some of the most common things kids hear are:

- "Your father/mother is mean to me."
- "Your father/mother doesn't love me anymore."
- "I'm not getting what I need."
- "I don't feel wanted anymore."
- "I'm not good enough for this family."

These reasons are really a way of saying that the people in a marriage have changed. Often, these changes cannot be easily avoided. Sometimes it may seem as if one event caused the change in a marriage. But most often, hurt feelings and unhappiness have been there for a long time.

Living in an unhappy family is painful. If problems and unhappiness last for years, they can cause great suffering for everyone. Sometimes divorce is really the best way to end the unhappiness.

You Feel the Tension the Most

Unhappiness and tension ruin a family. Parents as well as children do not have their needs met. They just feel stressed out all the time. That puts you in a very difficult position. You cannot take sides because you love both parents. So you are in the middle.

Dear Diary,
Mom and Dad fight all the time. Every day. Every night. Sometimes I can't get to sleep. And I am too embarrassed to have friends over. I do not like to hear Mom and Dad call each other names. And I really feel scared when they ask me who is right. Nobody is right. I love them both. I can't say one is right and the other is wrong. That would be taking sides. I wish they would just go back to being happy, but I don't think that will happen. I used to like having dinner together. Now nobody talks. We just eat in silence. How can I be happy when people I love are unhappy?

Clarence, age 16

When your parents fight, it upsets everything. You count on your parents for many things. And those things are different when there is tension and anger in the house.

You need to rely on things being the same every day. You count on Mom or Dad to buy food and prepare meals. You depend on Mom or Dad to drive you to places that you need to go. And you need Mom and Dad to spend time with you. But

Knowing they can depend on their parents makes children feel secure.

When parents argue, children often feel afraid and confused.

when a marriage has problems, all of those things
can change. You may not know how to act. You
may be afraid to make matters worse, so you avoid
your family altogether.

Trying to Hide Conflict

Your parents may try to hide their troubles from
you. They think that if the family *looks* happy they
will *be* happy. They try to act happy. Then one day,
without warning, it all blows up at once. It hits you
suddenly. Then you are angry and shocked. You
may not even believe it.

Your parents' troubles may be so bad that they
can't be hidden. But you may still try to ignore
them. You may pretend they don't exist. It is too
painful for you to think about what might happen.

Divorce May Be the Best Answer

Divorce is not always a bad thing. Sometimes
all efforts fail and a marriage just does not work.
This is often hard to accept at first.

Sometimes a mother and her children are being
beaten, abused, or threatened. In that case, the
need for separation and the decision to divorce may
be more obvious and welcome.

Many people see divorce as a way to end their
unhappiness. But the decision is never easy, and
both parties may not always agree. It is always
hard to think about changing your life. But in the
long run divorce may be the right choice.

You Need to Know about the Divorce

It is very hard for your parents to tell you they are going to be divorced. They know you will meet the news with tears and begging. You will be frightened. You will be angry, too. You may offer bribes to your parents. You may try to make a deal. You may promise to be good if your parents stay together. But *your* behavior cannot keep their marriage together.

You may get into a panic about moving. Maybe you will be upset about losing friends and changing schools. Most of all, you may be saddened about losing a parent when one moves out.

Still, your parents should tell you when they are having serious problems. They should not let the idea of divorce come as a complete surprise. Your parents should let you know what to expect. That way, you will not fear the worst. You will see that it's not the end of life. By explaining the divorce to you, your parents let you know that they are think-ing about you, too. Not just themselves.

When you are not told what is going on or what to expect, you may imagine things on your own. You may have a completely wrong idea about the reason for the divorce. You may think it's because Dad had trouble holding a job. Or maybe it was because Mom wanted to go back to school. Even worse, you may think it was something *you* did. That is why it is best for your parents to let you know as much as possible, as soon as possible.

Moving away can be a frightening experience for a child.

Parents Divorce Each Other, Not Their Children

Your parents are not going to divorce because of you. Parents divorce because *they* have problems. They may have problems with each other, or with themselves. You may think that your parents are rejecting you. Perhaps you think that you haven't been "good enough." Regardless of your own behavior, no child can prevent a parent from feeling unhappy in a bad marriage.

Common Fears and Emotions

Dear Diary,
Yesterday Mom told me she was going to divorce Dad. They have yelled at each other a lot. This last week was very bad. They never stopped yelling. I am scared. Mom says Dad is moving away. He's moving to another state. He is leaving us alone. I am afraid I will never see him again. I hate him. I hate them both. Now we won't have any money. And I won't be able to go out with my friends anymore. If we have to move, I will die. I hate moving. I don't want to leave my friends. I don't want this to happen.

Michelle, age 15

The fears that Michelle expresses are very common. You may have heard yourself say the same kinds of things. You will need to tell your parents about your fears. Perhaps they can help you to see that things will work out in time.

Remarriage and Change

It is never easy when a parent remarries. The new marriage can be upsetting for many reasons. For you, remarriage ends a dream. The dream that your natural parents would get back together. That is why remarriage is often met with anger.

Remarriage also changes your relationship to your parents.

You may have been already torn between your natural parents because of a divorce. Now a third parent is added, and perhaps another child. And that means a new set of feelings. And a new set of problems.

You may use your anger to make your new stepfamily unhappy. Stepparents are easy targets for anger. You may make things hard for your stepparent. You may misbehave. You may not cooperate. You hope your parent will take your side and find fault with your new stepparent.

THINK ABOUT YOUR FEELINGS

1. Do you remember being unhappy before your natural parents divorced? How unhappy were they? Can you see any good things about the fact that they separated?
2. Do you blame yourself for your parents' divorce? Are you confused about why they got divorced? Have you asked your parents to explain some of their problems to you? Have you asked them to let you know what to expect?

Chapter 4

When Death Changes a Family

It takes many things to make a stepfamily work. But one thing is the most important of all. The family members must understand one another's feelings. Each member must see what makes the stepfamily special. Then each member can understand the special feelings involved. Talking openly is always best. Discussing feelings is a good way to solve problems. It is also the best way to avoid problems.

Something has to happen before a stepfamily begins. A family changes or ends. The breakup of a family is very painful for all its members. A first family is not forgotten just because a stepfamily begins. It takes time to get used to the loss of a first family. It takes time to adjust. You cannot be happy until you have adjusted to the loss.

When a Parent Dies

Stepfamilies are often formed after the death of a parent. The surviving parent is forced to raise the children alone and to adjust to being a single parent. After some time has passed, the surviving parent may be ready for another long-term relationship. Sometimes it can lead to remarriage and the creation of a stepfamily.

The greatest loss for you is the loss of a parent. Your parents are the most important people in your life. Parents offer love. They give security. Parents give you a feeling of stability. That means that you can rely on things staying the same. Stability is very important.

A parent teaches you how to act. A parent shows that when you give love, you get love in return. This is a basic part of living. A parent is also a role model to teach you how to behave. You learn how to act by watching your parents.

Parents give you encouragement that helps to strengthen your self-esteem. Even if you feel scared about the future and the choices you will have to make, you believe in yourself. It is also important for you to know that someone is there to advise and support you.

The whole family is greatly disturbed when a parent dies. The daily routine in the family ends. Everything that seemed normal and natural now has to be planned and changed to meet the needs of the family unit. Nothing is as it used to be.

When a parent dies, family life changes very suddenly.

Feeling Guilty

Dear Diary,
This is the first day I can write in my diary again. I stopped writing because my dad died. He was killed in a car accident. It happened two weeks ago. I have been crying for the last two weeks straight. Mom has been crying, too. And so has my sister Jenny. I cannot stop thinking about Dad. His things are everywhere in the house. Like his chair at the dining room table. I asked Mom not to take his chair away. She said she wouldn't. I don't get why Dad got killed. He was the best driver. He was always strong. I feel bad that sometimes I upset him. Sometimes I think that maybe he was upset when he got killed. I think maybe I made it happen. I wish I had never made him angry. The day before he got killed he yelled at me. It was for not keeping my room clean. I don't think I can ever stop seeing Dad in my head. I keep seeing him the way he was. I wish he was still here. I am angry at him for going away. He left me and Mom and Jenny alone.

                                        Gary, age 14

You may feel guilty when a parent dies. You feel that maybe you caused the death. You think you did it by upsetting your parent. You also wish you had behaved better when your parent was alive. People cannot control death. Gary did not cause his father's death. Most teenagers who lose a parent feel that they could have been a better son or daughter for their parents. It is a natural feeling. With time, you will realize that your parent loved you. You will remember that you made your parent proud and happy. You will realize that you were accepted for your good points as well as any bad points. You were loved for who you are, not what you did or did not do.

Time to Mourn

It takes a lot of time to get over the death of a parent. It is one of the most upsetting things that will ever happen to you. You need time to be sad. The way you show your sadness when a person dies is called *mourning*. Often a part of mourning is feeling angry with your dead parent for leaving. Another part of it is deep sorrow because you can never see your parent again. Mourning also means adjusting to change. When your parent dies, life becomes difficult. Change can be very scary.

When a Widowed Parent Remarries

A woman whose husband dies is called a *widow*. A man whose wife dies is a *widower*. Parents who lose a husband or wife sometimes become especially close to their children while they are in mourning. You may take comfort in this closeness with your parent. He or she seems to love, care for, and protect you more than before. Therefore, you may be confused and unhappy when your parent decides to remarry in the future.

Dear Diary,

Everybody wants me to look happy all the time. Dad
is always telling me to smile. Mostly when we are
with my grandparents. But I don't feel like smiling.
I don't feel happy. Mom has only been dead for
eight months. I miss her. I feel like crying all the
time. But Dad says Paula will think I'm not happy
with our new family. People will think I don't like
Paula. She's my new stepmother. I like her all right.
But she will never replace my mom. I don't know
why Dad married her so soon. Didn't he love Mom as
much as we do?

                                                    Laurie, age 15

People often want children to act a certain way
when a stepfamily begins. Parents want to make
the new family work right away. They want everyone to be happy. They are eager for everyone to
love and accept everyone else. But those are not
fair expectations to have.

Feelings don't change overnight. And even if
your natural parent is loving, he or she may still not
understand your needs. Here are some unfair
things that you may be asked.

• *Stop frowning. It's over. Try to forget it.* A
parent may ask you to try to forget what happened
so that the new family can be happy. But that is too
hard for you. You can't just stop feeling sadness.
Sadness is a natural feeling. It can't be turned off.
It must stop over time.

There will always be reminders of a missing parent.

• *Stop crying. Be a man. Try to be grown-up.*
Sometimes your parent will ask you to stop *showing* sadness. That is also hard. Crying and feeling sad are very important parts of letting go. They help you to get used to a loss. Parents may want everything about a new family to seem perfect. They don't want to see crying or unhappiness. But feeling the pain of a death should never be avoided. People need to work through their grief.

• *What's wrong with you? You don't seem to care.*
Sometimes your parent may think you aren't crying *enough.* Your parent feels pain and wants you to feel the same way. Then he or she may say you don't care. That makes you feel guilty. But everybody deals with pain and death differently. Some people cry for months. Others do not cry at all. Others cry only in the privacy of their bedroom. All of those ways are okay.

• *Don't talk that way about your father.* You may
need to say out loud that you are angry about your
parent's death. Depending on how your parent
died, you may hold him or her responsible. For
example, it may be harder for you to mourn for a
parent who was a substance abuser or one that
committed suicide, than for a parent who had a
fatal accident. Some people may think your words
don't show respect for the dead. But talking openly
helps you admit that your dead parent had faults.
He or she was not perfect. When you accept the
truth about your dead parent and express your
feelings, you are coping with the death in a more
healthy way.

Making Things Work

For a stepfamily to work, all members must
understand one another. They must be aware of
what has happened. They must respect each
other's feelings. They must realize what other
members are going through. And must give one
another time to heal from the heartbreak or disap-
pointments in the past. A stepfamily can be happy
only when the parents and the children try to see
things from the others' point of view.

Things a Parent Cannot Get from You

It is important to remember that you cannot fill
many of your parent's needs. All your love and
friendship are not enough. Your parent may feel

lonely for other adults. Adults have feelings that you cannot understand. They have emotions that they cannot share with you.

Parents are likely to miss adult love and sex. Love and sex are very important for adults to share. Parents need closeness with other adults. They also need to feel attractive to others. They have been living without a husband or wife. Soon they may need to get back into the world, to feel that they are "still alive."

Most parents handle these feelings by starting to have dates. If they find someone they care about, they may want to remarry.

Loneliness and Hurt

You may feel very alone and left out when your parent remarries. You may feel that the adults in your life have now joined forces. You may feel that "It's me against them." You may also feel that you have no one to talk to. You may think that your natural parent won't want to hear your true feelings about the stepparent, especially if you don't have nice things to say. That makes it more difficult for you to speak truthfully.

A Stepparent Can Also Be a Hero

A stepparent doesn't have to be the "enemy." He or she can often be a real hero. She or he can make a child and a parent feel like a whole family again. A stepparent can provide the "missing

piece" that is needed to complete a family picture.
She or he can provide added security and love.
And a stepparent can meet the needs of the other
parent. These roles are worthy of respect and love.

THINK ABOUT YOUR FEELINGS

1. Do you think of your stepparent as a replacement
   for your first parent? Do you give your stepparent a chance to be herself or himself? Do you
   constantly compare your stepparent to your first
   parent?
2. Are you angry that your parent remarried? Can
   you accept the fact that the parent you live with
   needs adult companionship?

Chapter 5

Getting Used to Stepbrothers and Stepsisters

Any family situation has rough spots. Even the most "ideal" families have conflicts and problems to work out. Having stepsiblings (stepbrothers and stepsisters) is like any other part of family living. Some of it will seem easy and some of it will seem hard. The toughest problems usually develop when children are thrown together in a new family without enough time to get used to the situation. Often, this causes the family members to have unfair expectations of one another. And this can make people disappointed and angry.

Thinking about and discussing your expectations honestly may help you to understand your feelings. Sharing those feelings is probably the most important thing you can do in your new stepfamily.

Sharing a room with a new stepsibling is hard. It takes time
to get used to each other.

Jealousy

Stepsibs can become jealous of one another. Sometimes they are jealous of the attention their own parent gives a stepsib. Sometimes there is competition for a "special" place in the family. Who is the best in school. Who is the best in sports? There is always competition between brothers and sisters. Natural siblings have problems getting along, too. Sometimes the competition is healthy. It makes some people try harder than they might otherwise.

Different Children, Different Attitudes

Parents may treat one child as the "natural" child and the other as the "stepchild." But it is understandable that they need time to adjust to the new family as well. Some favoring at first cannot be avoided. Each parent has lived with his or her own child much longer. He or she is more sensitive to that child. The natural parent knows his or her own child's strengths and weaknesses. Each may favor that child without meaning to hurt or isolate the stepchild.

You may all have to learn new rules. Old rules may not apply in the new family.

Gaining Stepsiblings Can Be a Good Thing

Many children are happy to gain new brothers and sisters. Getting stepsibs has many good points.

Here are some of them:

• *A stepsib means a new friendship.* Sometimes it means the end of being alone. Stepsibs of similar ages are new companions.

• *A stepsib is someone you can relate to.* He or she is struggling, too. He or she understands the problems of being a stepchild and knows what you are going through. You can go through the family adjustments together.

• *Stepsibs can help each other understand step-parents.* Each can explain his or her natural parent to the other. This can improve the relationships for all the members of the family. Communication will be better, too.

• *When stepsibs get together, they can share.* They can share friends, toys, clothes, and many other things. This is often a great boost to both stepsibs.

Stepsibs Who Visit

Visiting stepsiblings can be more difficult to deal with. Because they are not around as much, you simply have less time to get to know them and work things out.

A visiting stepsib may resent the live-in stepsib. She or he may be jealous because the live-in step-child spends more time with the natural parent. Visiting stepsibs are also unsure of themselves. They are unsure how their real parent and the new parent feel about them. They may not feel they are part of the family they are visiting.

A New Baby and a Single Stepchild

Many remarried couples want to have children. When there is only one child in a stepfamily, a new baby can cause some uncomfortable feelings. Newborn babies need a lot of attention. They take up most of a parent's time. The stepchild can feel ignored.

The stepchild may feel that the baby is "more related" to the family and that he or she is "less related" and less loved. A stepchild may feel left out of the family. But parents can love more than one child at a time and fill the special needs of each. That is why the new parents should take extra care to show their love to both children.

Try not to confuse blood relationship with love. Remember that a blood relationship does *not* necessarily make someone love you any more or less.

THINK ABOUT YOUR FEELINGS

1. What are the good things about having new siblings? What are the things you and your stepsiblings can share?
2. How do you think your life will change when a new baby joins the stepfamily? What can you do as the "big brother" or "big sister" to help?

Teens and parents should discuss their feelings with each other.

Chapter 6

New Family, New Roles

As we have already pointed out, the creation of a new family is a major change for everyone. The members of a new stepfamily have usually had experience in other families. Their experience often makes them anxious to have their new family feel more like their old family. But a stepfamily will most likely never feel like the family you once knew. But that is not necessarily bad. In time, you may come to appreciate the special qualities of your new family.

Teens in Stepfamilies

The teenage years, also called adolescence, are a very difficult time to join a new family. This is a time when you are starting to feel many new and confusing emotions. Your body is changing fast.

57

You are starting to think about dating, love, and relationships. And you are trying to find an identity for yourself in the world. Joining a new family and living with new people can seem like too much to bear on top of all this!

As a teen, you may also be yearning for more independence. You may feel the need to spend less time around your family and more time with your friends. But a new stepfamily can place a lot of pressure on you to "be part of the family." And this added pressure can often be frustrating.

Teens Can Play an Important Role

Because of all the other pressures, a teen may feel "out of place" in a new stepfamily. But teens can actually play very important roles.

As a teen, you probably know more about the give-and-take of family relationships than younger children do. You can see your parents more clearly. And you can understand more about the cooperation needed to make a family work. Teens can help younger siblings cope with living in a new family. They can offer advice and comfort that no parent can equal. In this way, a teen can be a sibling's most important friend in the stepfamily.

A New Family Helps You to Grow

A new family does put a lot of demands on you. But learning how and trying to make a new family work can also make each of its members stronger.

It means that everyone must examine their expectations of one another and the family. There is no room to be totally self-centered. Each person in the family has different needs. And it often forces family members to take more time to communicate with one another. Once much of the adjustment work is done, however, you'll probably realize that you've become a better, happier person for being a part of your new family.

THINK ABOUT YOUR FEELINGS

1. Have you thought about ways you can help others in your family as well as yourself to cope with your new circumstances?
2. Have you talked to your parents about the parts of your new family that make you anxious or unhappy? Have you told them about your fears?
3. Write down your feelings on a sheet of paper or in a diary. Make a list of all the things that make you unhappy about your new family. Then make another list of all the good things about your new family. After you have thought about all those things, put your list away. Then later, when you feel upset or angry, take the list out and read it to yourself. Having your feelings down on paper is often a good way to deal with them.

Glossary—*Explaining New Words*

abuse Hurting someone else.

adolescence The time from puberty to adulthood.

adoption Becoming the legal child of another person.

biological Having to do with the body; natural.

compromise Agreement by meeting someone halfway.

discipline Training in good behavior.

favoritism Treating one person better than another.

frustration Feeling upset, discouraged.

grudge Long-lasting feeling of anger at someone.

guidance Showing someone the way.

guilt Feeling of being responsible for something.

identity Who a person is.

loyalty Being true to a person.

mourning The way we show grief or sorrow after a death or a loss.

rejection Feeling unwanted.

relation Member of the same family.

resent Dislike; feeling jealous of.

role model Person whose behavior is an example to others.

separation Moving apart.

sibling Brother or sister.

stepfamily Members of two families joined in one new family.

stepsibling Brother or sister related by marriage but not by blood.

wholeness Feeling of being complete.

widow Woman whose husband has died.

widower Man whose wife has died.

Where to Go for Help

Stepfamily Foundation
333 West End Avenue
New York, NY 10023
Telephone: (212) 877-3244

Stepfamily Association of America
28 Allegheny Avenue
Baltimore, MD 21204
Telephone: (410) 823-7570

**American Association for Marriage and
    Family Therapy**
1717 K Street NW
Washington, DC 20006
Telephone: (202) 429-1825

National Council on Family Relations
1910 West County Road B
St. Paul, MN 55113
Telephone: (612) 633-6933

For Further Reading

Berger, Terry. *Stepchild.* New York: Messner, 1980. This book is about the thoughts and feelings of a boy whose mother remarries. Problems and adjustments involved in being part of a stepfamily are discussed.

Berry, Joy. *Every Child's Guide to Understanding Parents.* Chicago: Childrens Press, 1986. Explains to children why parents do what they do and how to get along in a family.

Kaplan, Leslie S. *Coping with Stepfamilies,* rev. ed. New York: Rosen Publishing Group, 1991. Examines stepfamilies in detail. Discusses some of the problems that can arise in stepfamilies and how to deal with them.

Masoli, Lisa Ann. *Things to Know about Death and Dying.* Morristown, NJ: Silver Burdett Press, 1987. Talks about stepfamilies that form after the death of a biological family.

Raible, H. "The Stepsibling Shuffle." *Choices*, September 1987. Reorganization and adjustments for the children when a stepfamily is formed.

Index

About the Author
Bruce Glassman has authored over fifteen books for young adults and has been a staff writer on two Connecticut newspapers. He currently works as a book editor and a freelance writer and lives in Wallingford, Connecticut, with his wife and family.

About the Editor
Evan Stark is a well-known sociologist, educator, and family therapist—as well as a popular lecturer on women's and children's health issues. He is the author of many publications in the field of family relations and is the father of four children.

Acknowledgments and Photo Credits
Cover photo by Stuart Rabinowitz
Photos on pages 2, 8, 13, 14, 33, 34–35, 43, 52, 56: Stuart Rabinowitz; pages 19, 24, 38, 47: Blackbirch Graphics.

Design/Production: Blackbirch Graphics, Inc.